THE MIRACLE OF
ST. MICHAEL AT COLOSSAE

Leon of Mt. Athos

Translated by: Francois Nau, D.P. Curtin

THE MIRACLE OF ST. MICHAEL AT COLOSSAE

Copyright @ 2020 Dalcassian Press

All rights reserved. No part of this publication may be reproduced, distributed, or transmitted in any form or by any means, including photocopying, recording, or other electronic or mechanical methods, without the prior written permission of the publisher, except in the case of brief quotations embodied in critical reviews and certain other non-commercial uses permitted by copyright law. For permission request, write to Dalcassian Press at dalcassianpublishing at gmail.com

ISBN: 979-8-3302-6684-5 (Paperback)

Library of Congress Control Number:
Author: Curtin, D.P. (1985-)

Printed by Ingram Content Group, 1 Ingram Blvd, La Vergne, Tennessee

First printing edition 2020.

THE MIRACLE OF ST. MICHAEL AT COLOSSAE

THE MIRACLE OF SAINT MICHAEL THE ARCHANGEL AT COLOSSAE

Composed in Medieval Greek by: *Leon of Mt. Athos*
Original French Translation by: *Fr. Francois Nau*

I. Therefore, the beginning of miracles and healings and gifts and graces, which have been granted to us by the Lord through the grace and presence of the most blessed archangel Michael, had long ago been foretold and shown by the holy apostles Philip and John the evangelist. Finally, the blessed apostle and evangelist John, after completely expelling and eradicating the most abominable name of Diana from Ephesus, ascended to visit the holy apostle Philip. For he himself was also engaged in a great struggle against this very wicked beast. After the holy kiss, the apostle Philip indicated the snares that the same wicked Diana had plotted against him, and how he could not expel her abominable memory from the same city. Indeed, this bloody and wicked viper was the most evil of all serpents, surpassing the poisons of asps, and first among all harmful animals and reptiles, and surrounded from all sides by every deadly poison. The unhappy and wretched unbelievers worshiped her as a great goddess and adored her and sacrificed to her, ignorant of the true God. For frequently, while the holy apostle Philip was sitting and teaching the people, she would attack him greedily with suitable weapons, desiring to kill him, and she would cry out with deathly voices against him, saying, "Depart, Philip, from this city, before I cause harm to you and make you perish." But he, nevertheless, confidently preached the word of God to all the people and of truth, and an innumerable multitude was converted daily to the Lord.

II. Meanwhile, with both apostles pouring out prayer to the Lord, they immediately fled from her, emanating from Ierapolis. After this, the excellent and most pious heralds of truth hurried to a certain place called Reheretopa. Where, after a prayer was offered, the blessed John sat with the holy apostle Philip and designated the place, saying to the people: "For in this place there will come a great leader," Michael, to show here glorious and astounding miracles. Therefore, the holy apostles went out from there and traveled through the other cities preaching the word of God. And immediately in the aforementioned place, a bubbling spring of water emerged where countless miracles began to occur daily, and healings of various illnesses.

III. After the departure of the holy apostles, instigated by the devil, the unbelievers began to rage and tumult against the Christians again. With the passing of many years after the discovery of the aforementioned water, the daily rumor spread throughout the whole world of the miracles that were coming from the same sacred fountain, and many afflicted with various illnesses sought refuge there and were healed immediately. Also, a crowd of pagans gathered there, and seeing the healing of many illnesses, they believed in the Lord Jesus Christ, abandoning the error of idols, and were baptized. Meanwhile, there was a certain man in the city of Laodicea, a most pagan and idolater, who had a single daughter who was mute from her mother's womb. Her father decided to go to that water with many others, because many pagans were going there and being healed, freed from whatever illness they had. One night, the blessed archangel Michael appeared to him in a vision: Go with your daughter, he said, to where the sanctified water is shown, and by my name, if you believe, you will return to your home with joy. He immediately got up and hurriedly went with his daughter, and beholding the grace of God, he believed in God, and approaching those who were being healed, he said, "Tell me, I beg you, whom do you invoke when you pour the water over your bodies?" And they said, "We invoke the Father, the Son, and the Holy Spirit, and the intercession of the blessed archangel Michael." Then he raised his eyes and hands to heaven and said, "O Father and Son, and the Holy Spirit, who is one God, through the intercession of Saint Michael the Archangel, come to my aid, help me, a sinner. And when he had said this, taking the water, he put it into his daughter's mouth, and immediately her tongue was loosened, and the girl cried out saying, "God of the Christians, help me, truly your power is great, Archangel Michael." And that man was immediately baptized with his daughter and his whole household, and he built there a small chapel in honor and in the name of the blessed Archangel Michael, over the same holy water. And he returned rejoicing with his daughter to his house, glorifying and praising God. But the insane people, seeing these things, raged against the faithful, especially against the holy place, and they thought to overthrow it, trying to bury and exterminate the sanctified fountain completely from that place so that it would not even be named.

IV. Therefore, after ninety years from the construction of that holy dwelling which had been built over the aforementioned fountain, there came a certain man about ten years old, born of religious and Christian parents, named Archippus. He first began to live in the venerable temple of Saint Archangel Michael. For this boy lived a venerable life, living for sixty years after he began to serve in the aforementioned oratory, not eating bread nor drinking wine. Flesh never entered his mouth, nor did he ever wash his body. His food was wild herbs cooked without oil, and this only once a week. And his soul departed on the third day. He sustained himself with very little water for refreshing the body rather than for drinking. His clothing was a very rough cloak, and if it was not changed once a year, or if it fell apart due to extreme old age, he would wear it, covered with a hair shirt on top so as not to be seen by anyone. Moreover, at his head was a hair shirt wrapped in thorns, and in these the holy man would rest when the time for sleep came. He was diligent in night vigils of prayer, never allowing rest to his body, but subduing all its allurements, tormenting the spirit, and preserving the innocent and pure soul from the snares of the enemy. Embracing a narrow and difficult path, he longed with all his prayers for the heavenly homeland, persisting in prayer day and night, saying: "Do not allow me, a sinner, O Lord God, to prosper in this world even a little bit, nor let the pleasures of this world delight the eyes of my heart at all, nor let my body ever be persuaded to indulge in bodily pleasures, may my eyes not be lifted up to the fleeting glory of the world, but deign to fill them always with spiritual tears, and illuminate the secret of my heart with the knowledge of your most holy precepts, and grant me, a wretched spirit, the grace to give of yourself, which you have deigned to grant to all who have pleased you from the beginning. And he would say: "For what need is there to care for this body, which will soon be dust, a worm, and putrid matter. For the adornment and care of the body is the nakedness of the incorruptible soul. For the soul is the true beauty of the body. Therefore, these are the garments of the soul: true faith in God, nakedness and neglect of the flesh, lack of food and drink, angelic behavior, lying on the ground, special vigils, sighs and fountains of tears, repentance for past sins, quietness and almsgiving, humility and gentleness, patience and love, and other things which are pleasing to God. For in these ornaments the soul is delighted and rejoices. What else does the soul demand from the body but to live justly and soberly? Similarly, the body illicitly desires what belongs to it, the same belly's voracity, lust, greed, impurity, and all corruptible desires and useless cravings, in which the unhappy soul is caught and ensnared, and which sink mankind into ruin and perdition. Finally, what shall I, wretched one, do? Help me, O Lord my God, and crush in me the grain of mustard of bodily strength, give me a contrite and humble heart, so that I may not be confounded, nor despised by your immense mercy. For I, O Lord God, in the morning flourish like grass, in the evening I wither and dry up, but still I will not rest until my limbs, with your help, mortify those things which are above all carnal desire and pleasure.

V. Thus, the man of God Archippus meditated day and night, following an angelic way of life on earth, persisting constantly in praising God, giving thanks to the almighty God who granted him patience and long-suffering in all things. A multitude of Christians and pagans from all around gathered there, and as many as confessed the holy faith with fear of God and genuine faith. And they professed faith in the indivisible Trinity, saying: O Almighty Father, who with your only begotten Son and the Holy Spirit are one God, through the intercession of the holy Archangel Michael have mercy on us, and they poured that holy water over their bodies, and immediately they were healed from whatever illness they had. But the unbelievers and enemies of truth, refusing to see the glory of God from which they should have benefited, fell into worse depravity. For every single day they roared like lions, gnashing their teeth against that most holy place and striving with all effort to overthrow the oratory, to bury the life-giving fountain, and especially to slay the most reverent servant of God. Frequently, the most impious ones, coming cruelly, beat him severely with clubs. Others, taking wooden crosses from the oratory, broke them over his head in their fury. And others, pulling him out by the hair of his head and beard, cast him out and, devoid of all piety, beat him. But he, enduring all patiently, gave thanks to Almighty God in all things. Others continued to try to bury that life-giving fountain. But when they approached it, their arms and hands were immediately held. Others, desiring to approach, saw flames of fire coming from the same fountain towards their faces, and thus confused and half-burned, they turned back. And others spoke to each other, saying: If we do not bury this sacrilegious fountain, and that seducer is not extinguished, our gods will undoubtedly be despised by all, and their sacred worship will be reduced to nothing. And every day they inflicted excessive and most cruel punishments on the servant of God, Archippus, which he endured patiently, giving immense thanks to God.

VI. Moreover, in the same place there was a river flowing on the left side of the oratory, called Chrisis, and the enemies of truth tried with all their might to divert it from its course and mix it with the sacred spring of the oratory, only to eradicate the healing water from that place, but they did not succeed. For when they attempted to do this, by divine will the water of the same river began to flow here and there, so that it was divided into two parts. And one part that was divided turned towards another part, that is, towards the right side of the altar, and then flowed until the present day.

VII. Furthermore, there were two other rivers that came from the eastern parts, the passage of which was divided by three miles from the aforementioned sanctuary, one of which was called Lycocapros, and the other was Kysos. These rivers joined at the summit of a great mountain and, when united, descended on the right side of the same mountain and flowed in the regions of Litia. The ancient enemy and adversary of all goodness, the inventor of all evils, and the opponent of all who desire salvation, who, due to his pride, fell from heaven and wallows in filth, and transformed from an apostate angel, condemned to eternal fire, the antichrist, did not cease to incite the minds of pagans to overthrow the most sacred temple and the abolition of the holy water. Therefore, he instilled in the hearts of the wretched and they turned the aforementioned rivers against that most sacred place, so that it would be completely exterminated by the multitude of waters. The place was also suitable for the descent of waters, because, as already mentioned, the river ran down the sloping side of the mountain, and the place where the sacred oratory was located stood out a lot, as if the water of the river seemed to flow precipitously into it. Therefore, gathered from all cities and towns, an insane crowd of about five thousand men came to Laodicea, a crowd of wickedness, and they plotted vain things against the Lord and against Michael, the archangel of the highest divinity. And their leaders and blind guides of the blind addressed the people, saying: The place is suitable for the destruction of the temple of the wicked and for burying the sacrilegious water, because of whose evil deeds, the worship of our gods has been almost abandoned and destroyed. Therefore, let us come and force the water of these rivers against him from the height of the mountain, so that by the multitude of waters, all the power of wickedness may be completely exterminated from that place, through which the people are led astray every day. For we cannot otherwise kill that sorcerer and consign his ashes to the depths of oblivion, except by the rush of the multitude of waters and with the help of our gods.

VIII. Next to the sanctuary of the archangel, on one side of the oratory, there is a certain foundation of a marvelous size, in length and width below, beyond measure, and surrounding the oratory in front and back by about seventy cubits. The gatherings of the wicked and enemies of the truth approached. From the head of that rock to the summit of the highest mountain where the aforementioned rivers Kysos and Lycocapros met, they unanimously, digging, made a passage in the manner of a channel, so that these same rivers could deposit there to bury and destroy the place of God's sanctification. For the insatiable dragon and tireless adversary incited them. When this was completed and perfected, they blocked the mouths of the rivers so that they would not flow for ten days and so that a very abundant multitude of waters would gather for the overthrow of that most sacred place. And behold, the torrents were filled, and the hollows of the mountains were filled with the multitude of many waters.

IX. But Archippus, the servant of God, who was the steward of that most sacred place, seeing the diabolical operations and the disturbances and the madness of the profane people, threw himself prostrate on the ground, beseeching the Almighty Lord and the intercession of Saint Michael, so that he would keep that place unharmed and safe from the rush of waters, and for ten continuous days he did not eat or drink, nor did he rise from the place where he lay prostrate, but glorifying the Lord he said: Blessed be the Lord my God, I will not leave this place, nor will I retreat or flee, but I will die here from the onslaught of the incoming water. For I believe and trust in my Lord who will save me from a weak spirit and storm through the intercession of the most holy archangel Michael, who never forsakes his sanctuary, nor this place forever.

X. After ten days had passed, the most wicked and cruel beast came, and from all piety, they were foreign to the prepared riverbed against the Archangel of the Lord, saying to each other: Let us release the rivers and quickly depart, standing far away from a higher place rejoicing, so that we may see the extermination of that sacrilegious temple. And they stood on the left side and looked towards the south, showing each other the rush of water with a great roar descending from the height of the mountains.

XI. But the man of the Lord, Archippus, prostrated in the oratory with his face to the ground, wetting the floor with tears, incessantly invoking the Almighty Lord. And suddenly, touched by divine inspiration, he rose from the ground and began to sing this psalm: The rivers have lifted up, O Lord, the rivers have lifted up their voice. The floods have lifted up their waves. Wonderful are the surges of the sea, wonderful is the Lord on high. Your testimonies, O Lord, have been made very credible; your house will become holy, O Lord, for the length of days. When this was completed, a very loud thunderclap occurred; and the Archangel of the Lord, Michael, descended from heaven and stood at the head of that aforementioned stone, and he said to God in a loud voice: "Leave the oratory before the storm engulfs you, my servant." The man of God, Archippus, went out of the oratory and saw the shining face of the glorious archangel. He fell on his face on the ground as if dead. Then the blessed archangel Michael called him a second time: "Arise, beloved soul of God, and come to me." The holy man replied, "Lord, I am not worthy to come near you, for I tremble at the glory of your majesty and dare not approach." To which the great Michael said, "Do not be troubled or afraid, but rise to your feet." So he quickly rose and went to the oratory, trembling beneath the holy altar, and commended his soul more attentively to God. The angel of the Lord said to him, "Have confidence in coming to me, for behold, the roaring rivers are coming against you." And the servant of the Lord said, "I believe, my Lord, for the power of our God is great and of the magnificent archangel Michael, who does not allow this place to be destroyed until the end of the world." As the man of God left the oratory, the archangel said to him, "If you believe, servant of God, that God is able to guard this place and keep it safe from the onslaught of water, hurry to witness His power and might." Then the faithful servant of God, Archippus, approached and stood by his side on the left, hearing his voice but seeing the greatness of his glory. The archangel said to him: Do you know who I am? And the saint replied: I do not know, my lord, because I am shaken on all sides by strong fear. Then the prince of the heavenly hosts said: I am Michael the archangel. I am the one who stands before the sight of the Lord of all and cannot bear to look at the terrible and unsearchable glory of his divinity and the unquenchable light of his majesty, but you, terrified by the form of a servant and unable to bear his splendor, have wasted away as if consumed. How then will you contemplate the majesty of the almighty God, before whom I stand with trembling? Again the archangel of the

THE MIRACLE OF ST. MICHAEL AT COLOSSAE

Lord said to him: Do you see, holy man of God, the water descending from the heights of the mountains? And he replied: No, my lord, but with my ears I hear a great sound and the roaring of many waters. Do not be afraid, said the archangel to him, but stand undaunted, hesitating at nothing, and you will see the wonders of our Lord God.

XII. And behold, a great multitude of waters descended copiously from the heights of the mountains, with a tremendous roar and loud noise. But when it approached them, the most glorious and great prince of the Lord, Michael, raised his voice against the same rivers. Why do you hasten, he said, Kyse and Lyco-capre? Who has deceived you to come here, leaving your own channel? Saying this, he made a sign against the rush of the waters, then commanded with powerful words. Stop, he said, the water stood still in the same place and immediately stopped its rush. A truly amazing and greatly astonishing thing happened, after the unusual division of the Jordan. The water was finally raised up before the footsteps of the archangel like a mountain, a terrible sight! in height about forty cubits.

And the archangel said to the man of God, "Do you see, most just man, the power and might of God?" And he replied, "Yes, my lord." And the highest archangel said, "Therefore, do not fear the rush of these waters, nor be afraid."

And immediately, just as Moses once divided the Red Sea with an outstretched hand and a rod, so too the great prince Michael, the archangel of the Lord, extending his terrible right hand in a certain manner, struck the summit of that stone with the rod he had mentioned, which was immediately split and divided from top to bottom and down to the abyss. A loud noise was made in its splitting as if a hundred thunderclaps, and a great earthquake occurred throughout that land; indeed, a great chaos was made there, so that no man could see where it ended. Then the archangel of the Lord said to the blessed Archippus, "Do you see, man of God, the great wonders and the power of the Almighty?" And the saint replied, "Yes, my Lord, I see, great wonders and the power of the Almighty God working with you."

THE MIRACLE OF ST. MICHAEL AT COLOSSAE

He again stretched out his hand, signed that chaos, blessed it, and said, "In this place, all ailments will be healed, all infirmities, all ill health, and all evils will be eradicated, and all false appearances or the brazen chains of diabolical fraud, those bound here shall be loosened and their wounds healed, and from various infirmities they shall be transferred to safety. And whoever flees to this place and invokes the Father with genuine faith and truth, and the Son and the Holy Spirit and the intercession of the archangel Michael, by my name, shall not depart from here sad, but joyful and rejoicing shall return to their own. By the grace of God and my protection, this place will be sealed and safeguarded, kept safe in the name of the Father, and of the Son, and of the Holy Spirit.

But our enemies standing from afar, who look upon us, shall become as stones there, until the water of these rivers submerges and overturns my sanctuary. Those who immediately turn into stones, as a sign of His power, shall remain so until this present day. Therefore, he said to the servant of God: Turn, man of God, and stand at my right hand. And he immediately approached and stood at the right hand. Then, the archangel of the Lord turned towards the waters of those rivers and said: Cast yourselves into this whirlpool, and you shall be swallowed up, roaring and raging, flowing until the end of time, for daring to come against me. The glory and reverence of this most holy place will be through Jesus Christ our Lord. When the most glorious prince of the archangels had spoken these words, water began to flow with a great roar through the depths of that abyss, such that no man could see it at all, only the infinite sound as if coming from the depths. And once it had passed the place where the oratory was located, about the distance of an arrow's flight, it emerged again from the depths outward onto the earth. And thus, flowing through its own channel, it revealed to all how much angelic power had been at work there. Indeed, such great and magnificent things happen there daily.

Miracles are wrought, benefits and healings of various infirmities, so that no one may doubt that the angelic presence is constantly there, that our Lord Jesus Christ, through the merits and intercession of the most blessed archangel Michael, does not cease to work even unto this day, to the praise and glory of His name, to whom with the eternal

Father and the life-giving Holy Spirit be honor and glory, power and might through endless ages of ages. Amen.

The Scriptorium Project is the work of a small group of lay people of various apostolic churches who are interested in the preservation, transmission, and translation of the works of the early and medieval church. Our efforts are to make the works of the church fathers accessible to anyone who might have an interest in Christian antiquities and the theological, philosophical, and moral writings that have become the bedrock of Western Civilization.

To-date, our releases have pulled from the Greek, Syriac, Georgian, Latin, Celtic, Ethiopian, and Coptic traditions of Christianity, and have been pulled from sundry local traditions and languages.

www.ingramcontent.com/pod-product-compliance
Lightning Source LLC
LaVergne TN
LVHW052049070526
838201LV00086B/5184